The Adventure

Piper's Journey Home

The True Story of a Rescue Puppy

Dave Osborn

The Adventures of Piper Series
Piper's Journey Home
The True Story of a Rescue Puppy (Book 1)
© 2024 Dave Osborn

Adriel Publishing

SECOND EDITION

Printed in the U.S.A.

Cover design by Dave Osborn & Elizabeth Lawless

ISBN: 979-8-9897531-0-9

www.DaveOsbornBooks.com

Dedication

This book is dedicated to the American Dog Society along with the thousands of rescue shelters and Humane Societies worldwide that rescue abandoned and stray animals. The selfless work of their staffs and volunteers in finding these animals good, caring homes has greatly enriched the lives of their adoptive families.

Prologue for Parents

While **Piper's Journey Home** is a true story that has a happy ending, most rescue dog adoptions – particularly from shelters – do not work out as well. Statistics from the American Dog Society reveal that of all dogs adopted from shelters, an average just over 20% of them will be returned to the shelter within six months, and only 50% of those returned dogs will ever find permanent homes. New owners, or new dog "parents," are just not prepared for the time and energy required with raising a rescue puppy or retraining an adult dog.   They become frustrated and give up too soon.

Piper's Journey Home was written to educate both potential rescue adults and children on what it takes to have a successful adoption and to reduce the number of returned animals.   With patience and time, adopting a rescue dog or puppy can be a richly rewarding experience, and new adopting dog families will receive more love in return then they can comprehend.

6

Chapter 1

Homeless, Cold & Soaking Wet

It was cold and wet, and I was all muddy and soaked from the rain. As I huddled next to my mother, brothers, and sisters to try to stay warm, all I could think about was how hungry I was.

I think I found some plants to eat yesterday, but I'm not sure. My mother had very little milk for all of us, so we had to look other places for something to eat.

We didn't have a home, so we had to stay in ditches and sewers for shelter. I didn't want to go off alone to find food because there were raccoons around that would hurt me.

I ate whatever I could find, and I shared what I found with my brothers and sisters.

Sometimes we would find dead squirrels and birds, and we ate them just so we could stay alive. Many times these animals were spoiled, but we had to eat them – worms and all.

I didn't know how much longer I could stay alive.   I was sick, I felt terrible. I couldn't keep down what I ate, and I didn't have the strength to get up and walk. If a raccoon found me and wanted to hurt me, I could not protect myself.

Then I saw a lady nearby outside her house. If I could just reach her, maybe she would give me something to eat.

Chapter 2

A Break from the Cold and Wet!

Since I was so weak, I was too slow, and the lady got back to her front porch before I could make it to her.

Somehow I was able to give a weak bark, and she turned and saw me. She came over and petted me and took me back to her house.

It felt so good not be so cold. The lady cleaned up my paws and dried me off before giving me some food in a bowl.

That's when I saw that there were three other dogs nearby who were looking at me.

The food the lady gave me was really good, but I threw it all up within a few minutes. The lady was kind and cleaned up my mess and gave me water.

They had three large dogs and did not have room for another one.

The lady said she thought I was cute, and she would like to find me a home – a real home!

Chapter 3

A Small Chance at a Real Home!

Her husband agreed to keep me around for two or three more days – but that was all.

Meanwhile, I had a warm place to sleep and food that wasn't rotten or spoiled.

The lady came home the next day and told her husband that she had talked to a friend who might want to rescue a puppy.

Her family had once owned a dog but had not had one for several years and she thought they might like to have another one.

I couldn't believe my ears! The lady cleaned me up so I would look my best. When the friend came to meet me, she even brought her husband!

I knew then that I had a chance to have a home, and I was on my best behavior!

Chapter 4

I Get Lucky!

The friend, whose name is Marilyn, held me and petted my fur. I was still not clean, and I couldn't walk very well, but I was much better than when I first arrived.

Marilyn's husband, Dave, also held me and petted me. When Dave and Marilyn said they would take me, I was so excited and happy, I could only just whimper and cry for joy. I knew then I would live.

I thought about my brothers and sisters, but they went looking for food without me and were no longer nearby. I never saw them again.

Dave came to pick me up, and I was so excited to be going to a real home.

The minute I got in Dave's car, however, and it started moving, I threw up all over his front seat.

I was so afraid Dave would take me back and say he didn't want me, but he took me to his home and gently cleaned me up and then cleaned up his car.

I knew these were nice people who would take care of me and get me healthy.

The first thing Marilyn did when Dave brought me inside was to say, "Your name is now Piper, and you are our new puppy!"

Chapter 5

I Finally Have a Home!

Dave gave me my first bath in a big sink, and for the first time in my life, I felt clean. It felt so good.

Marilyn poured a bowl of water for me while Dave filled a bowl with dog food. It was so good even though some of it came back up.

Later that day, Marilyn gave me a rib bone with a little meat on it then took me to their back yard - it was wonderful!

I still didn't feel good, so Dave took me to a veterinarian nearby named Dr. Shelly Mitchell. She checked me out and wasn't happy with what she learned about me.

Dr. Shelly told Dave that I was starving and had worms in my tummy from eating rotten food. The worms were getting all the healthy food I had eaten, so nothing was left for me. I only weighed 16 pounds. She said I should weigh around 30 pounds if I were healthy. Dr. Shelly then gave Dave lots of pills and medicine and told him how often to give them to me, and that I would get better soon.

I started feeling better the next day. I was a little stronger and could stand up and walk better. I didn't throw up my food that day, and I started to grow again.

I began to feel good for the first time ever, and it was really nice to have a warm, dry place to sleep at night. After about a week, the worms were gone, and I didn't throw up anymore.

I quickly came to love Dave and Marilyn for rescuing me and giving me a wonderful home.

Chapter 6

Things I Had to Learn in
My New Home

One of the first things I had to learn was not to go potty in the house. Out in the ditch it didn't matter where I went to potty, but living in a house is different.

Dave took me to a spot in their back yard and taught me to potty there. He would take me out there many times each day, and very soon I knew that's where I should go potty.

One day I needed to potty, and Dave hadn't taken me out to the potty place yet, so I barked and went to the patio door.

Dave was happy with me for letting him know I needed to go potty, and he quickly opened the patio door for me and took me out to my potty place.

From then on, when I needed to potty, I would just bark at the patio door, and Marilyn or Dave would open the door for me. I knew what to do after that all by myself.

Every morning Dave and I go for a walk. It helps me to build strong muscles and legs. Sometimes we see the neighbors and talk with them, and I am used to walking with Dave on a leash.

I really like it when we see children walking to school nearby because they always want to pet me, and I love being petted by the neighborhood children!

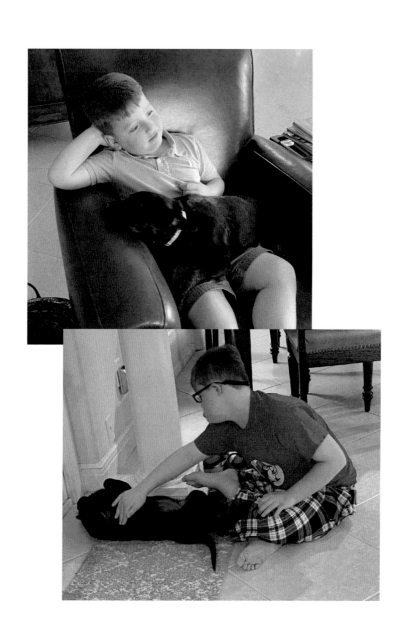

Chapter 7

I Meet the Family

I met Dave and Marilyn's grandsons – Welles and Joshua – who came to visit for the weekend with their parents Matt and Dara.

Matt is Dave and Marilyn's son and Dara is their daughter-in-law. They were nice also and seemed glad to meet me.

Since Joshua and Welles are young like me, we had a great time getting to know each other.

Welles took me for walks with Dave and also brushed my fur to make it soft and smooth.

Joshua spent lots of time petting and playing with me. I was so happy to meet more of my new family.

I learned to love Joshua and Welles, and they learned to love me as well!

I also met Jaime, Dave and Marilyn's daughter. She is a teacher. That is someone who helps others learn.

Jaime teaches little kids and she told me she often reads books about dogs to her students. Maybe one day she will read a book to them about me!

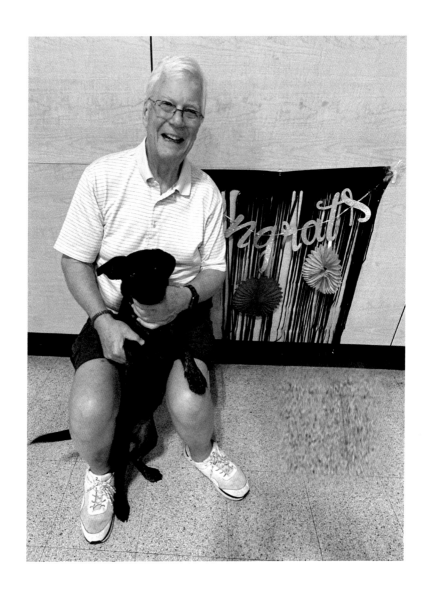

Chapter 8

Puppy Kindergarten

Dave signed me up for some puppy training at a local pet store.

It was scary at first. We went to a big building, with bright lights and lots of shelves. I wasn't sure what it was at first but Dave explained it was a store that had lots of stuff for dogs, cats and other pets.

Dave said we would go to a special place in the store called "puppy kindergarten. "It was great fun, and I learned to "sit," "get down," "stay," "wait," and "leave" things. I was so proud when I graduated!

Dave was also pleased but said I still need to go to "puppy middle school" to learn not to jump up on people when I meet them and to learn how to do a better job walking on a leash.

It will be fun, and I can't wait to go!

Chapter 9

I Learn Who I Am

Dave ordered a test kit and took a wet sample from my mouth with cotton on a stick. He then sent the stick off in the mail, and I learned that he was having me checked to see what kind of dogs my parents and grandparents were.

The answers came back, and it seems I have several different types of dogs in my doggy family!

My closest family member is a German Shepherd. German Shepherds are often highly intelligent, good with children, protective, and are good workers. Yes – all those things are like me!

My next family member is a Chow Chow. Chows are usually clean, easy to housebreak, do not have much doggy odor, and are very loyal and protective. Yes – all those things are like me, too!

My next family member is an American Pit Bull Terrier. People have found Bull Terriers to be playful, stubborn, devoted, energetic, and mischievous. I like to get into mischief, too!

Finally, my last family member is a Labrador Retriever. Labrador Retrievers are known to be lovable, affectionate, good with children, good with other dogs, and energetic.

And you guessed it – all those things are like me as well!

When Jaime, Dave and Marilyn's daughter, saw the report, she laughed and said, "that's why Piper has one ear up and one ear down! Her "up" ear is her German Shepherd ear, and her "down" ear is her Labrador Retriever ear!"

This makes me look different from any other dog in the world, and I love it!

Chapter 10

More Time With Dr. Shelly

A few months later, Dave and Marilyn took a vacation and needed a place for me to stay while they were gone. They made plans for me to stay at our veterinarian's boarding kennel, and they took great care of me while they were away. I love Dr. Shelly. We get along great!

I was really glad to see Dave when he picked me up, but I also enjoyed my time at the kennel.

While I was at the veterinarian's kennel, Dr. Shelly "fixed" me so I will not have puppies. She also put a "chip" in my shoulder so if I get lost, whoever finds me will be able to call Dave or Marilyn to come and pick me up.

I love my home and neighborhood, so I do not ever want to get lost.

Chapter 11

I'm Doing Great Now!

I am growing like I should now. I eat healthy food, earn a treat every day and sleep without worrying about raccoons. I have reached my normal weight and now weigh forty-nine pounds!

I get my walking exercise every day, and I run around my back yard several times each day. I could hardly walk when I first got to my new home, but now everything is much better.

I earn my room and board by protecting my new home, and I do an excellent job every day! Life is good now!

I am a very lucky dog, and I love my new home!

I cannot wait for my next adventure – going to therapy dog school to learn how to help people who need comfort and help just like I did when I was younger.

But that is another story!

Dave Osborn

As a retired business executive, Dave is following a life-long passion of writing and has several projects in mind for future online and offline publications.

He also has a passion for dogs so be sure to look for more books about his adventures with Piper, his companion and rescue dog.

Dave is also on the Board of the American Dog Society.

Dave enjoys South Texas bird hunting and bay fishing and is an avid grill master. Additionally, he is a bluegrass music fan and enjoys playing the piano, guitar, bass, and five-string banjo. Another favorite pastime is sailing, and Dave holds both U.S. and International sailing certifications.

Dave holds a Bachelor of Science Degree from Stephen F. Austin State University in Nacogdoches, Texas, and a Masters of Business Administration from Texas Christian University in Ft. Worth, Texas.

He resides in Harlingen, Texas, with his wife Marilyn and rescue dog Piper. They have two adult children and two grandsons who reside in the greater Houston area.

Author's Acknowledgements

While my name is on the cover, I could not have written this book without the help of the following:

- Marilyn Osborn, former Senior English teacher and later Dean of Students and Head of School, for her help in sentence structure, wording, and ideas for photos;

- Jaime Osborn, kindergarten teacher and reading specialist, for her help with leveling the vocabulary and sentence structure;

- Matt and Dara Osborn for their many reviews and suggestions on making chapters for the milestones;

- Joshua and Welles Osborn for their help in keeping Piper busy while the rest of us worked on the book;

- Dr. Shelly Mitchell, Arroyo Veterinary Hospital, for her good care in getting and keeping Piper healthy;

- And last but not least, Piper Osborn, who is the best companion imaginable!

Made in the USA
Las Vegas, NV
06 December 2024

12724999R00036